The student guide to computer science C++

The student Guide to computer science C++

Sam Chae

Writers Club Press
New York Lincoln Shanghai

The student Guide to computer science C++

Writers Club Press
an imprint of iUniverse, Inc.

For information address:
iUniverse, Inc.
2021 Pine Lake Road, Suite 100
Lincoln, NE 68512
www.iuniverse.com

ISBN: 0-595-18739-0

Printed in the United States of America

For Jenny

Contents

Preface xi
    Techniques Used in This Book ....*xii*
    Is This Book For You? ....*xii*
    An Overview of the Material in This Book ....*xiii*
Chapter 1: Basics 1
    Object Oriented Programming *1*
    Brief History *3*
    C++ Compilers *4*
    The 4 Important Rules of C++ *7*
    Spacing *9*
    Chapter Summary *10*
    Before You Begin *10*
Chapter 2: Your First Program 12
    Your Very First Program *12*
    Include Statement *13*
    The Main function *14*
    cout *16*
    Commenting *17*
    Chapter Summary *19*
Chapter 3: Declaring Variables 21
    What are variables? *21*
    Math with variables *24*
    Math shortcuts in C++ *27*

Chapter Summary *28*

Chapter 4: cin 30

Chapter Summary *31*

Chapter 5: Naming Convention 33

Chapter Summary *34*

Chapter 6: Loops, if else, and Program Flow 35

The Comma (,) Operator *35*

for Loops *36*

if else Statement *39*

while Loops *44*

Nested Loops *45*

Summary: Chapters 1–6 ....*46*

Chapter 7: Special Characters 48

The \n Newline Character *48*

endl *49*

Tab Character *49*

Error Beep Character *50*

Quotes *50*

Chapter Summary *51*

Chapter 8: Functions 52

return *55*

Returning Functions with Multiple arguments *57*

switch Statement *59*

Chapter Summary *61*

Chapter 9: Global Variables 63

Chapter Summary *65*

Chapter 10: Arrays 66

Arrays *66*

The Matrix Array 67

Chapter Summary 68

Chapter 11: Structures 70

struct 70

Chapter Summary 73

Chapter 12: Classes 74

The Class 74

Why Classes? 77

Derived Classes 78

Constructor and Destructor 80

Chapter Summary 82

Chapter 13: Pointers and Memory Allocation 83

Memory and C++ 83

& 85

new and delete 87

Array Pointers 89

Chapter Summary 89

Chapter 14: const, Namespace, and the ? Operator 91

Compiling Separately 91

using namespace std; 92

? Conditional Operator 93

const variables 93

Chapter Summary 94

Chapter 15: Strategies in Comp Sci 96

Knowing Your Language 96

Math Problems 97

Subject Matter Problems 98

Bigger Programs 99

Putting It All Together *99*

Practice Problem 1 ....*100*

Practice Problems *103*

Chapter Summary *104*

Chapter 16: Debugging 106

Commenting Your Code *107*

Warnings *107*

Careless Mistakes *108*

Memory Leaks *108*

Chapter Summary *109*

Glossary 111

Index 125

Preface

C++, by far, is one of the most powerful and widely used computer programming languages ever created. Not only has it become the basis of tens of thousands of careers, but it has also become something so important, it's taught in almost every school in this country. And when you do end up taking a computer science C++ class, either it be at your high school or college, you're in for a bumpy ride. For some people, the concepts of object oriented programming (more on that later) seems to falls right into place. While for others, it can be something that is so difficult that it makes no more sense than a pad of chicken scratch. No matter which group you fall under, this book will be teaching at a steady pace for beginners, and as more of a reference and study tool for more advanced students, especially ones enrolled or are planning to be enrolled in computer science. This book is written to help you improve in your course, and build a solid foundation to work with in the future. By the time your done with this book, you will know the fundamentals and many more advanced topics of the C++ programming language Being able to make your own programs and zip through your computer science course in a snap.

Techniques Used in This Book

This book is not made for specific types of people only. This book is designed to be compatible with most types of students. Also, the examples in this book are not too closely related or connected together. That is, I'll never write an example in this book that is continued from the previous chapter, because that would be a waste of time for someone that doesn't have too much of it. Nor will I be using long complex examples because they merely confuse the reader and not help towards understanding a concept. I will be keeping examples and code as simple as possible so that anyone could understand them.

Is This Book For You?

This book was not written to target specific types of students. This book is very general and can be used by the following types of people:

- Students that currently are or are planning on enrolling in a **high school** or **college** computer science C++ course. This includes all courses involving the C++ programming language, particularly a first course or second.

- Someone that has programmed before but wants to brush up on certain things.

- Anyone in general that would like to learn the C++ programming language for the first time. No previous programming or computer knowledge is necessary.

If you fit into any of these categories, this book is for you. This book assumes that you have never programmed before. But even if you have previous programming experience, you can still read this book. It will strengthen your programming skills and may introduce you to some new ones as well. For students in computer science courses, this book can be a great way to study for your final exam, or as a reference to look at when programming or even doing homework.

An Overview of the Material in This Book

In this book, you will learn all the materials and then some, for your computer science C++ course. These include C++ basics, structure, Object Oriented concepts, variables, classes, keywords, loops, memory management, functions, return statements, algorithms, common computer science course materials, arrays, structures, data writing and reading, inheritance, and much more. Don't be overwhelmed; this book will teach you as painless and easily as possible. Although I recommend you read the entire book from start to finish, you may also skip ahead chapters if you wish to do so, since no chapters are based directly off the preceding.

Chapter 1: Basics

Welcome to the wonderful world of Object Oriented Programming! This chapter is dedicated to teaching you the basics of C++. Like a little bit of history and some general knowledge about programming. You can skip this chapter if you are already familiar with the concept of Object Oriented Programming. But it couldn't hurt to brush up on some basics though, especially for you CS students.

Object Oriented Programming

As you should have guessed, C++ is an *Object Oriented* programming language. OOP for short. OOP is the basis for the C++ programming language, so you should have a good understanding of it. First off, you know that the reason for writing code is to solve a problem. Pretty much all code is written with the same general purpose: to solve a problem of some sort. OOP is a type of code that is written to specifically solve that problem and nothing else. It is actually quite simple. Imagine a shoe with shoelaces tied really tight. Now imagine a foot. The problem is: *the foot will not fit into the shoe.* This is obviously because the shoelaces are tied too tightly together. Now, you must write code to solve this problem. A non-object oriented programming language would approach this situation by trying to force the foot into the shoe by pushing

1

and squirming. Eventually the foot would slip into the shoe, but that is after much unneeded energy, time, and effort are wasted. Even though it was really hard, it still solved the problem. It got the foot into the shoe and that's all that matters, right? Wrong. Even though you did get the foot into the shoe, you wasted more time than was needed to do so. I mean, wouldn't it be easier to just untie the shoe and then slip the foot into it? It would save more time and effort. This is exactly what object oriented programming does. It specifically solves the problem the best way it can. This is done by the code revolving around the problem, instead of having the problem revolve around the code. This is one of the main reasons that OOP is such a useful and flexible tool.

Another major part of OOP is its support for reusing code. In many programming languages, code must be typed and retyped to reuse it. But in OOP, the code is written once, and then recycled. This is a big deal for programming because it saves so much time and effort; a very important quality, especially at the professional level. This relates to another big part of OOP; *polymorphism*. Polymorphism is a way to have the program "think" in a way and use a certain type of object (more on this later), depending on what the circumstances are. This is also a very powerful tool in C++ because it allows the programmer not only to save time, but also to write code more efficiently and safely.

The last big thing about OOP is it's emphasis of hiding data, or storing it until it is needed. This is called *encapsulation*. C++ likes to hide, or encapsulate, data because when data is exposed, it can be improperly accessed, which leads to corrupt data. This is not a good thing, especially when your program is specifically made to handle large amounts of *important* data. It's like having a key to your home. You don't want strangers walking in and out of your house, that's why only you and your family members have the key. Like in OOP, only certain parts of the code can have the "key" to data, which makes everything much more safe.

Brief History

A big chunk of history can be credited to computer programming languages. With all the names, dates, and accomplishments, a whole book could be written about the history of computer programming. Although there were many languages developed, and still around today, C++ definitely stands out in the crowd. With its new concepts and ideas so different from the traditional ways of programming, C++ has become extremely popular since it's introduction in 1980. If you spare the details, the history of the C++ language is pretty simple. In 1970, *Ken Thompson* developed the B language at Bell Labs during his development of the UNIX operating system. Then in 1973, *Denis Ritchie* of Bell Labs added onto the previous B language and developed the C language. This language was written off of the B language with new additions and improvements. It was not until 10 years later, in 1980, that *Bjarne Stroustrup* of Bell Labs created a new language on the foundation of C, called C++. Accredited by its parent, the C language, C++ became very popular and seemed to have it's own distinct personality over other programming languages. Ever since then, C++ development has exploded all across the world. With tons of companies and corporations competing and making money from this object oriented programming language, it is definitely something for the record books.

C++ Compilers

A compiler is something that is used to build programs in C++. Without a compiler, a page of C++ code would just be a page of C++ code. It wouldn't do anything; you might as well just type the code into your word processor. The code can't become a program until you use a compiler to compile the code. For example, let's say C++ is a foreign language, like Chinese. Not everyone can speak Chinese, so they need some way to interpret Chinese into something that they can understand. When you write code in C++, the compiler "translates" the code you have written into a program. The program can then be used and be understood by people that don't know C++. Thirteen pages of C++ code are useless unless it is compiled because otherwise, it's just a page of code and doesn't do anything. For example, let's say that you made a program that counts from 1 to 10. The code would look like this:

```
#include <iostream>
using namespace std;
int main()
{
        for (int i = 1; i < 11; i++)
        {
                cout << i << endl;
        }
        return 0;
}
```

(Don't worry about understanding the code above. It's just an example.)

"Wow, look at that. It's C++ code. What am I supposed to do with it? All I see is just some confusing letters and words that don't make any sense. It looks impressive, but it doesn't do anything." This is what almost anyone looking at this code would say. But when the compiler "translates" this code, it would look more like this:

1

2

3

4

5

6

7

8

9

10

Now do you get it? The compiler translates the C++ code into a readable form. Into a program. But it's not that simple. Sometimes, there can be errors in the code. Maybe I misspelled a word or left something out. Then the program will not "translate." Instead, in the middle of the "translation," the compiler will notice the error, and will stop and you will get some message that tells you what is wrong. In most compilers, including the one you will probably be using in your computer science course, after you finish writing your code, you would select the button or menu item that says *COMPILE*, and use it to compile your code. What this does is the exact thing that we have been talking about. It "translates" the code. When you click *COMPILE*, it tells the compiler, "Ok, the code is done. Now I want you to check through my code. Make sure everything is OK, and if it is, translate it!" In your computer science course, all your code will be typed up in a compiler. It will look like a word processor on your computer, but with a bunch of cool gizmos.

The *debug window* is the part of your compiler where those errors we talked about earlier, are presented. If the compiler finds an error in the middle of "translating" your code, it will stop "translating" and the debug window will list all the errors that were found. Most compilers will even give you the exact location of the error. If you are a little unclear, you can also try this out if you have access to a C++ compiler. Identify the COMPILE button. It's most likely under a menu labeled *BUILD*. But even if you don't have access to a compiler, it's ok. You now know what a compiler does and how it works. This is probably going to be the second or third thing you will learn in your computer science course. Now that you know, you're already one step ahead. You're off to a good start.

The 4 Important Rules of C++

In C++, there are many different rules. Some you should know, and some you can just look up. The following three rules are very general rules that all C++ programmers should never forget:

- All code written in C++ is case sensitive! So, in your compiler, if you typed **main,** it would NOT be the same as **Main.** The compiler sees them as totally different things that have nothing to do with each other. If you have ever programmed in other languages like BASIC, you probably aren't used to this. But that's ok. Just remember that C++ is case sensitive, and your set.

- A **semicolon** (;) follows almost every line of code written in C++. In many cases, when code has errors, it is because the programmer forgot to put the ";" at the end of a line of code. But in some special cases, no ";" is needed. This will be explained in more detail later.

- The *source code file*, or the file where all your C++ code is written, is always saved with a "**.cpp**" extension. So "**MyCoolProgram**" would be saved as "**MyCoolProgram.cpp.**" And all *header files*, or the file that defines all the stuff used in your source code, always has a "**.h**" extension. So "**MyCoolHeaderFile**" would be "**MyCoolHeaderFile.h.**" I'll explain a little bit more about source code files and header files later, but for now, just know that *source code file=.cpp* and *header file=.h* and you'll be fine.

- { } (**brackets**) surround almost all of your code chunks. For each chunk of code, they are surrounded by { }. So if you have a paragraph of code, they would be surrounded by brackets. Although this isn't always the case, just know for know that { } are very important.

Spacing

In C++, spaces are not counted as code. It doesn't matter how the code in C++ is written because the compiler just reads the code, not the spaces. Remember, the compiler is nothing but a program that translates C++ code. It doesn't think or have a brain. When you get down to it, the compiler is actually pretty stupid. Therefore, your compiler doesn't care how sloppy or ugly your code is written. If you wanted, you could write code like this:

```
#include <iostream> using namespace std; int main() { for (int i=1; i < 11; i++) { cout << i << endl; } return 0;}
```

But this would only make the code complicated and hard to read. That is why C++ is usually written like this:

```
#include <iostream>
using namespace std;

int main()
{
        for (int i = 0; i  < 10; i++)
                {
                                cout << "Look! I'm looping!\n";
                }
        return 0;
        }
```

You don't have to space it exactly like this. This book will be spacing the code like this because that is what your code in computer science course will look like. Also, it is easier to read. Don't worry, most C++ compilers do this for you. Also, it doesn't matter if the code is not continued on one line. For example, if a line of code runs too long and skips to the next line, it doesn't affect the code, as long as the code is correct. But this is also something you should try to avoid unless it is absolutely necessary.

Chapter Summary

This chapter got you started into the wonderful world of C++ programming! You have learned about the compiler, the main device for writing code in C++, some brief history of the C++ language, some important rules, and the ever-important spacing rule. These rules will all be followed from here on out in this book so keep them in mind. Remember that spacing in C++ doesn't really matter. And keep in mind the four important rules you learned about in this chapter, as they apply to this book a lot. In the next chapter, we will be writing out first program.

Before You Begin

Before you begin, take a minute to clear you head. You shouldn't be reading this book, or any other programming book, in a noisy, hectic place. Go some place quiet and relax. This book will move at a very steady pace starting from the most basic elements of the C++ programming language. Ready?

Chapter 2: Your First Program

In this chapter, you will learn how to make a very simple C++ program using the most common functions. This first example will be very similar to the first one that will be done in your computer science course. It will teach you how to output text to the screen. It may seem a little bit difficult at first, but by the end of this chapter, you should understand it fine. I am going to give you an example, and explain every line. Don't try to understand the code in the example until I explain it. Let's begin.

Your Very First Program

We want to make a program that displays **"Hello"** onto the screen. It is actually quite simple. Here is the code to do this:

```cpp
#include <iostream>
using namespace std;
int main( )
{
        cout << "Hello";

        return 0;
}
```

Ok. Now don't be overwhelmed. When you compile the code above and run it, it looks like this:

Hello

Pretty easy huh? Ok now comes the fun part. I'm going to explain this code above line for line. Ready?

Include Statement

Ok, in the example above, look at the first line that says **#include <iostream>**. What this is called is an include statement. All C++ code is begun with the include statements. The include statement is sort of like a direction sheet for the source code. You see all the code under **#include <iostream>** ? If **#include <iostream>** wasn't there, none of the code under it would work. It defines all of the stuff used. Without it, the compiler wouldn't know what any of the stuff under it was. EVERY source code file in C++ uses an include statement. Typing **#include <iostream>** in the beginning tells the compiler, "Ok! I'm ready to program. But before I program, I want to tell you all of the keywords and functions and stuff that I'm going to be using in my code! All this info can be found in a file called iostream.h!" The **<iostream>** is a file that is the core of the C++ language. Almost all the code that you write for your computer science class will be using iostream.h. You get it now? **#include <iostream>** tells that compiler that I want to

INCLUDE all the stuff in the iostream.h into the file. The include statement is usually put in the first line of the code, or around the beginning of the code. Although you don't necessarily have to, it is better form. And form really counts, especially in computer science class. Oh, by the way, you don't have to use iostream.h. In some cases, you can use other files instead, depending on what specific stuff you are going to be using in your code. You can also have more than one include statement. It doesn't matter what order as long as they're all there. You could do it like this:

```
#include <fstream>
#include <string>
#include <dos>
```

This would use all the information from **fstream.h, string.h, and dos.h,** in your code. Oh, and the reason **iostream.h** is surrounded by < > is because it HAS to be. All header files, must be surrounded by < > in the include statement. Unless you made the header file yourself, than instead of < > you would use " ". But let's not worry about that now. Now we can move onto the next line of code.

The Main function

The *main function* is the second line of the previous code example. Let's look at the whole line:

int main()

This is called the *main function*. The *main function* is exactly what the name suggests; it is the MAIN part of the code. All C++ code has to have a *main function*. All the main code is placed in the *main function*. You should notice that this line starts off with the word **int. int** is a declaration for a variable or a function (more on this later), don't worry about it for now though. A function is a big chunk of code that is surrounded by { } (brackets) and in between those brackets, is code. You should notice that the directly after the *main function*, is a set of brackets. These brackets tell the compiler where the *main function*s code starts, and where it ends. The { brackets tell the compiler, "the code starts here!" And the } bracket tells the compiler, "the code ends here!" So everything in between the { } brackets is part of the *main function*. Like I said before, every C++ source code file has to have a *main function*. And it has to be called main. Not Main or MAIN. Remember, C++ is case sensitive. Now that we have covered the **int** part and the **main** part of **int main**( ), let's move onto the ( ) part. The ( ) parenthesis are like the { } brackets in a way, they signal the start and end. Remember that { } brackets hold code, but the ( ) do not hold any code. Instead they hold *arguments*. Arguments are explained later but for now, just remember that in a function, in this case the *main function*, the ( ) parenthesis hold arguments and the *main function*

MUST be in every program. Now your ready to move onto the 2 lines inside the { } brackets, which are:

cout << "Hello";

return;

Ready? Let's examine these two lines.

cout

cout is a function that you will be using constantly when programming, especially in your computer science class. *A function*, which will be explained later, represents a big chunk of code. And instead of re-typing that big chunk of code, the programmer can just type the function instead. cout is a function that is a part of iostream.h. Remember that an include statement INCLUDES all the info in iostream.h into your program. And cout is part of the info in iostream.h. So without iostream.h, you can't use cout, because you will get an error. Anyways, the purpose of cout is to display text onto the screen. Whenever you use cout, it is followed by << because << means OUTPUT. When you type << after cout, it tells the program, "Ok! I want you to output whatever is after the << onto the screen!" And since "Hello" is after the <<, the program will output "**Hello**" onto the screen. Get it? First off, you need cout to use <<, and when you use <<, whatever comes after << is what is displayed onto the screen. Oh yeah, and the ; is there because, like I mentioned earlier, lines of code have to have a ; at the end, to signal that the line of code is finished.

The reason that the include statement, the *main function*, and the brackets, don't have a ; after them is because include statements, brackets, and functions never have ; after them. It is just another rule of C++. You will feel more comfortable about this rule by the time you read more into this book. You can ignore **return;** for now. I will get back to that later. Oh yea, cout is pronounced CEE OUT.

Commenting

Almost all programming languages have some way of keeping the code organized by inscribing notes and comments. That is why it can't be stressed enough, the importance of the programmer adding their own comment in their code.

For example, if a programmer writes 30 pages of code, it would be incredibly hectic. Unless there were comments in the code that describe it and explain certain parts of it, it would be very hard to read it or edit it later on. Especially when the code is being read by someone else, or it's code that you haven't looked at in 3 years, In C++, the way to add comments into your code is by preceding the line with //. Doing this will make whatever follows the // into comments.

The compiler will merely ignore the comments, so it won't effect your code. Look at the example:

// these are comments....
//these comments help keep
//the code organized and
//more readable

The only thing about the // is that it makes only one line into a comment. But what do you do if you want to make a lengthy comment, and don't want to put dozens of // marks in front of all the lines? Just start the comment off with /* and end it with */. Like this:

/ This whole paragraph is a comment.*
It will be ignored by
the compiler. Usually, professional
code has a paragraph
like this before the include
statements, stating copyright
*info and the company name */*

You will have to use this for your code written in computer science class because the instructor will want to see your comments and notes. Comments should always be used, especially to keep your code more organized. In most compilers, comments will appear in a different color than the rest of the code, so it will be easier to spot and not make the code harder to read. Comments will be used in this book from now on.

Chapter Summary

Ok that is basically it. It may not seem like it, but you have just learned a LOT; about the first weeks worth of your computer science course. Let me sum up everything in this chapter. Include statements have the form: **#include < header files name goes here >**. It tells the compiler what functions and stuff you are using. Remember, unless the compiler knows what functions and stuff you are using, it can't use them. So the include statement is a must for all C++ programs. The header file, or the file that goes in between the **< >** in the include statement, is the file that hold all that info about the functions and stuff. Also remember, that the *main function* is a must for all C++ programs, and it is the main part of your code. The heart of your code. **cout** is a function that displays text onto the screen. The **<<** operator is used after cout and whatever come after **<<** is the text that will appear on the screen. So **cout << "Hel" << "lo";** will display **"Hello"** onto the screen. Brackets { } signal the start and end of a chunk of code, and ( ) parenthesis signal the start and end of arguments for a function (more on that later). Don't worry if you are a little confused about brackets and parenthesis, the examples in this book will help clarify them.

Well, you got through the first chapter. If you didn't understand anything in this chapter, re-read it. You must know this chapter because you will be using the stuff from this chapter in your computer science class, definitely.

Chapter 3: Declaring Variables

This chapter is a very important one that I would recommend everyone to read, unless you are already familiar with the C++ language. The reason that this chapter is so important is because it discusses variables, a huge part of C++ and your computer science course. I recommend you memorize all the vocabulary in this chapter, which will be *italicized*. Let's begin with some general info about variables like what they.

What are variables?

Ok. Right now, I want you to memorize the number 7. You have just stored a *value* in your memory. Variables in C++ work the same way. Imagine a variable as a box. You can put stuff in the box, but not ANYTHING you want. You can only put certain things in each box, according to what is written on the top of the box. So if I took a marker and wrote PAPER ONLY on a box, you can only put paper in it. This is similar to variables. Look at the following example:

```
int var;
var = 10;
```

A variable is declared in the first line. The variable's *identifier*, or name, is **var**. And it is a type int, or *integer*. Let's refer back to the example about the boxes. We have a box, a.k.a. **var**, and it has int written on it. So that means you can only put stuff in the box that is an int. And in the next line, **var** is *assigned* the value 10. Remember that **var** is like a box. In the second line, we are putting the integer 10, into the box. This is called *assigning* a variable.

A summary of the code example might help you understand a little better; an int, or *integer* was declared. This new integer was given the name **var**. You can name it whatever you want. Using letters, numbers, or _ symbols. **var** is then assigned the integer 10. So now, **var=10**. This is a fundamental of C++ that many students have trouble understanding. Perhaps an example will clarify it:

```cpp
#include <iostream>
using namespace std;
int main()
{
        int b;
        b = 7;
        cout << b;

        return 0;
}
```

Look at the code above. A new variable is declared. This variable is given the name **b.** Then, **b** is assigned a value of 7. So now, **b** is a box, that has "**int**" written on it, and it is holding 7. Then we simply use cout, to display variable **b**'s content, which is 7, onto the screen. When compiled, the output looks like this:

7

See? Isn't that simple? Your just declaring a variable called **b**, then assigning 7 **to b.** Then you just use **cout** like in the last chapter, and output it onto the screen. No problem. What's even better is, you don't always have to declare a variable as a type int (int=integer.) Variables can also be string of text, a letter, and even decimals. The following table lists variable types used in C++:

Variable	Example	Description
int	4	Non-decimal number positive or negative.
float	4.5	Any number including decimals.
double	400.5	Like float, but can be much larger.
char	b	A single alphabetical letter.
string	"Hello You"	A string of text.
long	40000000	A much larger int

So if you substituted **int b** in the previous example with **string b**, you could only assign a string of text to **b**. Or if you used **char b;** instead, you can only assign it one character, like "**Z**."

Also, there is another type of variable; *bool.* If you create a bool, or *Boolean* variable, the value can only be TRUE or FALSE. Or you can use 1 to represent TRUE, and 0 to represent FALSE. This will be unneeded until you get into loops and stuff later, so don't worry about it too much for know.

Easy stuff right? You have just learned one of the most important fundamental of the C++ programming language and already covered about 4 class periods in computer science. Let's move onto math using the variables we just learned in this chapter. Remember, the next chapter will be dealing with variables, so if you don't quite understand them, try re-reading this chapter.

Math with variables

One of the most useful reasons for using variables in C++ is for math. It is an easy concept to grasp. But in order to do so, you must know the symbols for addition, subtraction, multiplication, and division on your keyboard. The signs are the same as on a graphing calculator. + is obviously the sign for addition, and—for subtraction. Multiplication is *. So 5 * 4=20. And the sign for division is represented by /. So **10/5=2**. Look at the following example:

```
#include <iostream>
using namespace std;
int main()
{
        float a;
        a = 7.1;


        float b;
        b = 1.1;

        cout << a + b;

        return 0;
}
```

You will notice that the variables **a** and **b** are each assigned a value. The values assigned are both decimals. This is ok because **a** and **b** are declared as a float. Now cout is used to output the result of **a** + **b**, or 7.1 + 1.1. When you run the program, it will display:

8.2

onto the screen. You can use any of the other mathematical signs to do equations like this. If you had **cout << a * b;** instead of **cout << a + b;**, **a** and **b** would be multiplied, instead of being added.

Oh yeah, there's also another operator, less commonly used, called the *module,* or the % operator. This displays the remainder of two numbers. Thus, **10** % **3** =**1**, because **3** goes into **10** 3 times, and has a REMAINDER of **1**.

Also, you remember from math class what < mean. It is the less than sign. This can also be used in C++ when comparing things (more on this later). See the table below for the complete list of mathematical sign and comparing operators:

Sign	Example	Description
<	2 < 5	Less than sign. 2 is less than 5.
>	5 > 2	Greater than sign. 5 is greater than 2.
=	5 = 5	Equal to sign. 5 is equal to 5.
<=	A <= 5	A can be less than or equal to 5.
>=	A >= 5	A can be greater than or equal to 5.
==	A == 5	Comparing 2 values.
!	4 != 5	Not true. So != would mean "not equal to"
&&	A && b	If A is true, and B is true. Means AND.
||	A||b	If either A or b is true. Means OR.
+, -	1 + 2, 2 - 1	Addition, subtraction.
*, /	2 * 4, 4 / 2	Multiplication., division.
%	10 % 3 = 1	Find remainder of.

You are going to see these operators a whole lot in this book. Make sure you have a general idea of what they are. Throughout the book, you will gain better knowledge about them, so don't be too worried about understanding all of them now. Also, you'll be using them all the time to do formulas and stuff in your class. So get used to them. You can just flip back to this chapter and look at the table when you need to.

Also, make a note that if you try to set the value of an **int** to a decimal, it will automatically round to the nearest decimal point. For example, if you declared an **int** as **100.3**, it would be rounded down to **100**.

Math shortcuts in C++

C++ is filled with many shortcuts and steps that shorten time spent on programming. One area of many shortcuts is the mathematical portion of C++. Since there is so much math in C++, many shortcuts have been developed to shorten development time. For example, if you wanted to do this: **a =a + 7**, you could just write this instead: **a += 7**. They do the same thing. As for subtraction, the same form is used, but instead of the + sign, us a—sign, like so: **a -= 7**. This is also true for division and multiplication. This is just another thing that makes C++ all the more convenient.

Another shortcut in C++ is the **++** *operator*. Instead of doing **a + 1**, you can just do **a++**. The **++** operator, or the *increment* operator, adds 1 to whatever number is being incremented. Just by adding two plus signs after the variable. And likely, the—(two minus signs), or *decrement* operator, subtracts 1. That's how C++ got its name. It is C plus 1. Or C++. By the way, it doesn't work for multiplication and division. ** and // won't do anything. Well, // does do something, but that will be explained a little later. For now, make sure you understand some of these shortcuts because they can save you a lot of time. Also, almost everyone uses these shortcuts when the situation arises. So keep these shortcuts in mind throughout the rest of this book. They will be used in the examples.

Chapter Summary

This chapter dug a little bit more deep into C++. You have just been introduced to a lot of stuff; variables, math operators, and comparison operators, to name a few. You learned how to declare a variable by using keywords such as int, string, char, etc. Remember that when the variable is declared, you are creating something that holds a value. You can assign that variable with whatever you want. Of course, the value has to match what you declared it as. So if you declared an int, or integer, you should assign it an integer. If your variable is declared as a string, you should assign it a string of text. Also, keep in mind the operators you were introduced to in this chapter. You learned about the math operators, which are also used in many other languages, such as BASIC. You also learned that by using the math operators, you are able to do calculations in your code. You can use either numbers or variables in math equations in your code.

Chapter 4: cin

This short chapter will be outlining and explaining *cin*. cin is a function that is the exact opposite of the cout function. Although cin and cout both are defined in iostream.h, they do the exact opposite things. For example, cout *OUTPUTS* data, but cin *INPUTS* data. And cout uses <<, but cin uses >>. The << represent the *insertion operator* in C++, and >> represent the *extraction operator.* You should definitely know that because it is extremely important. << is output, >> is input. Remember that! It's very important because it doesn't apply only to cin and cout.

The reason for having cout is obviously to display data. But no one wants a program that just displays data onto the screen; that would be pointless. The reason cin is there is so that the user can interact with the program, and enter in information, which the program can use. The following example demonstrates cin and cout in action:

```
#include <iostream>
using namespace std;

int main()
{
        int age;
        cout << "Please enter your age: \n";
        cin >> age;
        cout << "Wow, your only " << age << " years old!";

        return 0;
}
```

The above example uses the same things we have been using all along. After the #**include <iostream>** and "**using namespace std;**" which will be explained later, there is the usual *main function*. Now everything so far should look familiar. You should notice some differences. Notice that after the first cout statement, there is a **\n** at the end of the sentence. This is a special *newline* character. When used in a string of text, it skips to the next line. These will be described later.

After "**Please enter your age:**" is displayed, it skips down to the next line, where cin is used so that the user can type in their age. After you type in your age, and press ENTER, the int variable named **age**, will be assigned the value of whatever the user types in. So if the user typed in 30, then age=30. The next line simply outputs your age in a sentence. Then the return statement, which is also discussed later. This code demonstrates an extremely easy example an important aspect of programming called *user interaction*. User interaction, like it sounds, allows the user to interact with the program and change outcomes by inputting his/her own data. User interaction is very important in any program. Remember that user input is the way that a user can communicate with the program.

Chapter Summary

In this chapter, you learned about the most commonly used input function used in C++, cin. Your CS class will definitely be using this and it will probably be the first or second thing you will learn after cout. Using cin is a great example of user interaction, because it allows the user to interact with your program and input data, changing variables and the way your program handles data. Make sure you have a good understanding of cin. It is a pretty big thing in any comp sci class. Also, don't forget that cin is pronounced SEE-IN, and cin is part of the iostream.h class, as is cout. Without including iostream.h into your code, you cannot use cin or cout. Because the iostream class defines them.

Chapter 5: Naming Convention

In C++, code can become extremely long. So long that it would be easy to get lost. For example, let's say you have 200 pages of C++ code. You declared a variable, MyVar, somewhere in the 200 pages. You could easily forget what you declared MyVar as. It could be an int, string, char, float, long, whatever. That is why there is a common naming convention in C++. These help keep track of what kind of variable each one is. Look at this table:

Character	Example	Type
n	nVar	int
l	lVar	long
d	dVar	double
f	fVar	float
sz	szVar	string
c	cVar	char

So a variable of type int, would always start with "n." A variable of type string would start with "sz." And so on. This book will use this naming convention from here on out. Because this is an important aspect of organizing your code in C++, and because it is so widely used, we will adapt to it as well.

Chapter Summary

This chapter was pretty straight forward. It just taught you a way to keep your code organized. When you programs become bigger, naming your variables with things like X and NUMBER and STUFF, just won't cut it. Using these prefixes in front of each variable, like nX, nNUMBER, or nSTUFF, will let you know at a glance, what kind of variable it is. This book will be using these prefixes so watch out for them. You should also use them when programming, not only because it is good form, but also because it will help you and make your code more organized.

Chapter 6: Loops, if else, and Program Flow

Loops are an extremely important tool to developing code in C++. It is also the main reason why code doesn't have to be 10000 pages long. First off, let's define loop. A *loop* takes code, and keeps executing that same piece of code as long as a certain condition is true. A keyword for doing loops are *for*, and *while*. Let's start with some basics.

The Comma (,) Operator

As I have mentioned before, C++ is filled with shortcuts. Another very common one that you will learn in computer science is the comma operator. The comma operator is equivalent to the word "and." Look at this example:

```
int nNumber1;
int nNumber2;
```

By using the comma operator, the code above can be shortened into:

int nNumber1, nNumber2;

As long as the variables are of the same type, they can be declared in the same line. In this case, all the variables are integers, so they can all be declared on the same line. You can even do this:

int f=1, e=2, x=4;

for Loops

While programming in C++, you may be confronted with situations that require repetitive tasks to be performed more than once. For this, the **for** keyword is used to create a loop that executes code repetitively. The keyword **for** is a main part of the C++ language. It saves time, effort, and is a great form of re-using code. Here is the basic setup for a *for loop:*

```
for ( set the variable ; as long as this condition is true ;
do this)
{
      code to loop
}
```

It's actually pretty simple. Let's look at the first part of the arguments, or the part in parenthesis, following **for**. You must have three things for a for loop, and they are placed in the parenthesis and separated by ; marks. First, you must set the variable. This means setting the variable you are going to use to a certain number, usually 0. Then you need to use the variable, that you set in the first part, to do something. The loop will continue until this condition is false. But as long as it is true, it will do something. Perhaps an example may help:

```
#include <iostream>
using namespace std;

int main()
{
        for (int i = 0; i  < 10; i++)
                {
                        cout << "Look! I'm looping!\n";
                }
        return 0;
        }
```

In the example above, look at the line that reads **for (int i = 0; i <10; i++)**. Let's examine the code in this line. Look at the first part of the loop:

int i=0

This called the *loop initialization*. The variable **i** is set to zero. You may have noticed that **i** is declared and assigned a value in the same line. Instead of doing 2 separate lines, **int i;**

and **i=0;**. This is another shortcut in C++ that is commonly used, it is the programmers choice whether or not to do it like this. The next part,

i < 10

is called the *loop test*. As long as this statement is true, that is, as long as **i < 10**, the next part:

i++

or the *loop update*, will execute. So as long as **i < 10**, **i** will increment. Each time **i** is incremented, one cycle of the loop is finished, and it will keep looping and incrementing **i**, until **i** no longer is **< 10**.

When the code above is compiled, the result is:

Look! I'm looping!
Look! I'm looping!
Look! I'm looping!
Look! I'm looping!
Look! I'm looping!
Look! I'm looping!
Look! I'm looping!
Look! I'm looping!
Look! I'm looping!
Look! I'm looping!

The program loops until **i** no longer equals to **10**. Every time the loop is executed; **i** is incremented. So eventually, **i** will become greater than **10**. And when this happens, the loop stops. I know this is a hard concept to understand. It takes some time to get used to this. The best method I suggest is to try building some of your own programs with loops. But if you don't have access to a compiler, just bear with me, and you will understand it eventually. If you are still having trouble understanding this, try re-reading the section above. Not everyone gets it after reading it through only once. Keep in mind that you just read everything you need to know, but your brain hasn't quite processed it yet. So try re-reading it. You definitely need to know loops, especially for your computer science course.

if else Statement

The *if else* statement is another powerful tool of the C++ programming language. Although it is not really a loop, I am including it here because learning this first will help you understand the other types of loop, the *while loop*.

Anyways, the *if else statement* combines a sentence-like form of coding with the ability to have an outcome be dependent on another. Basically, an *if else* statement checks something, and IF that something is so and so, then do this. ELSE, do this instead. An example should clear this up:

```
#include <iostream>
using namespace std;

int main()
{

        int nNumber;

        cout << "Please type in the number '3' and press ENTER
        cin >> nNumber;

        if (nNumber == 3)
                cout << "Good job. You typed 3.";


        else
                cout <<       "No, you were supposed to type 3!";



    return 0;
    }
```

In this example, a variable, **nNumber**, is declared as an int. Then cout is used to tell the user to type in '3' and hit enter. Obviously, after that, cin is used so the user can type in a number. Ok, this is where the loop comes in. IF **nNumber** == 3, then display "**Good Job. You typed 3**." But what happens if the number typed in by the user is NOT 3? This is what the else statement is for. ELSE, display "**No, you were supposed to type 3!**" When compiled, the output looks like this:

Please type in the number '3' and press ENTER
3 <ENTER>
Good job. You typed 3.

And if you type something else, rather than 3, it looks like this:

Please type in the number '3' and press ENTER
9 <ENTER>
No, you were supposed to type 3!

Get it? If **nNumber** is 3, then do so and so, but if **nNumber** is something else, do this instead.

You may have noticed some things that are different in the previous code example. First, you should notice that there are no brackets { } surrounding the 2 cout statements after if and else. This is another shortcut in C++. If the body in a loop is only one line, like in the previous example, you do not need brackets. This is because the compiler will assume the body code is the line directly following. But if the code is MORE than one line, you MUST have the brackets in.

Another thing you might have noticed is the two equal signs used in **if (nNumber == 3)**. The ==, remember, compares something. In the previous example, it is comparing **nNumber** to 3. If there was only ONE equal sign, like **nNumber=3**, then it would be *assigning* nNumber's value to 3, not comparing it. Be careful about that. Always keep in mind that == compares something, and = by itself assigns a value.

So far, we have only seen the *if else statement* with two choices. IF or ELSE. But what if you wanted more choices? Easy; just add more if's. But for every additional *if* that is used after the first one, you use *else if,* instead of just *if.* Look at this example of using multiple *if*'s:

```cpp
#include <iostream>
using namespace std;

int main()
{
      int nNumber;

      cout << "Please type in '3', '4', or '5' and press ENTER \n";
      cin >> nNumber;

      if (nNumber == 3)
            cout << "Good job. You typed 3.";

      else if (nNumber == 4)
            cout << "Good job. You typed 4";

      else if (nNumber == 5)
            cout << "Good job. You typed 5";

      else
            cout <<        "No, you were supposed to type 3, 4, or 5!";

return 0;
 }
```

In the previous example, more *if* options were added. So you would get a different response from the program for typing 3, 4, or 5. Not just 3, like the first example. See how flexible C++ is?

Whew! We've just covered a huge amount of C++. If any of this doesn't make sense to you at anytime, go back and read it again, slowly and more carefully. Remember, all the stuff you need is right here, and you might have to re-read it sometimes to get it through your head. Next, we are going to examine the *while loop*. This should be very simple, since you know now how the *if else statement* works. They are very similar so this next section should be a piece of cake.

while Loops

The while loop, in my opinion, is the easiest loop of them all. It executes a piece of code, while a certain condition is true. WHILE this is true, DO this. Look at this example:

```cpp
#include <iostream>
using namespace std;

int main()
{

        int nNumber = 0;
        cout << "Enter a number:\n";
        cin >> nNumber;

        while (nNumber > 0)  // while statement
        {
                cout << nNumber << " loops left!\n";
                nNumber--;
        }
                return 0;

}
```

The previous example uses a while loop to determine if **nNumber**, which is typed in by the user, is bigger than zero. If it is, then while **nNumber > 0**, it uses cout to display onto the screen, how many loops are left, and then decrements **nNumber**. It keeps doing this until **nNumber** is no longer greater than 0. At this point, the loop simply stops. Here's the output:

> Enter a number:
> 6 <ENTER>
>
> 6 loops left!
> 5 loops left!
> 4 loops left!
> 3 loops left!
> 2 loops left!
> 1 loops left!

Remember that the while loop, in this case, is comparing to see if **nNumber** is GREATER than 0. So if you put in a number LESS than 0, like a negative number, the program would simply skip over the loop.

Nested Loops

For complex and larger programs that require larger tasks to be performed, there is something called a *nested loop*. In my opinion, I don't think that the nested loop should even have a name. It's nothing more than a loop inside a loop. Simple right? It doesn't even need an explanation. A nested loop is a loop inside another loop. That's it.

I also want to talk about the old *infinite loop*. An infinite loop, like it sounds, is a loop that goes on forever and never ends. Especially in *for* loops, try not to initialize the loop with stuff that never ends. For example, **for (int x=8; x == 8; x=8)** would be an infinite loop, because x will always equals 8! It doesn't change the value of **x** or anything, it just sets it back to 8. I don't think anyone would make a mistake as silly as that, but infinite loops can be hidden or unable to be spotted so easily, so watch out for them.

Summary: Chapters 1–6

Congratulations! In these first 6 chapters, you've learned OOP, fundamentals major of C++, math and operators, cin, cout, loops, and various shortcut methods. You have covered a big chunk of your computer science course already! You're off to a great start.

The next example will be using cout, cin, a math operator, a comparison operator, a loop, and a variety of the fundamentals that you have learned ever since the beginning of this book. If you can understand the following code, you're all set. If not, go back and re-read parts that don't make sense to you, because I will NOT be explaining this code for two reasons. One, you need to test what you do and don't know, and two, it will help you assess your knowledge of the material covered so far. Try to identify all of the things used in the following example.

Everything in the next example was learned in the first 6 chapters of this book, so everything should look familiar. Here it is:

```cpp
#include <iostream>
using namespace std;

int main()
{
        int nInput, nInput2;
        char cYesOrNo;

        cout << "Welcome to number magic!\n";
        cout << "Enter any number\n";
        cin >> nInput;
        cout << "Enter another number.\n";
        cin >> nInput2;

        cout << "You picked " << nInput << " and " << nInput2 << "\n";
        cout << "Multiply them together? Type Y or N.\n";
        cin >> cYesOrNo;

        if (cYesOrNo == 'Y')
                cout << "The answer is " << nInput * nInput2 << "\n";

        else if (cYesOrNo == 'N')
                cout << "Goodbye.\n";
        else
                cout << "Please type Y or N\n";
        return 0;
}
```

Chapter 7: Special Characters

Earlier, you saw "\n" in action. This, as you recall, is called the newline character. When placed in a string of text, it moves down a line. Or creates a new line. There are many characters like the newline in C++. Some of them are rarely ever used, and some, you can't program without. This book will cover only the ones that you will encounter in your computer science course, which is already more than you'll probably need to know.

The \n Newline Character

As you should already know, the **\n** character, or *newline* character, is used to make a new line. If you compiled the following code without a \n character like so:

```
cout << "Welcome";
cout << "to";
cout << "C++";
```

the output would look like this:

WelcometoC++

The \n character can be placed anywhere in the string, not only at the end. Although some prefer to use the \n character for new lines, there is yet another way to do so.

endl

Another method for a newline character is by using *endl*. The only difference is that endl is a little bit easier to write because you don't have to include it in the string. It looks like this:

```
cout << "Welcome" << endl;
cout << "to" << endl;
cout << "C++" << endl;
```

It would produce exactly the same result as using \n. From here on out, this book will use endl instead of \n newline character.

Tab Character

Used in the exact same way as \n, the \t *tab character* creates a tab in the string. Adding \t to your string makes the same space as pressing the TAB button on your keyboard. This character is used in the same way as the newline character.

Error Beep Character

By using the **\a** speaker beep character, your computer speaker, or pc speaker if there is no sound card, will give off the default error beep. This is useful for indicating errors or getting the users attention. This is also used the same way as the newline character. Keep in mind that this character should not be used too much because it will give your program an unprofessional look.

Quotes

C++ is filled with many keywords. One that is used very often are the " " quotes. They go around strings of text. But what do you do if you want to include a quote in a string? If you did this:

cout << "So he said, "Hi my name is Bob," and shook my hand.";

The quotation marks are colliding. The compiler would see **"Hi my name is Bob"** separate from **"and shook my hand."** To fix this problem, inside of the string, use a \" to start the quote and \" to end it. Like this:

cout << "And he said, \" Hi my name is Bob, \" then shook my hand.";

When compiled, it would end up like this:

So he said, "Hi, my name is Bob," and shook my hand.

This is the best way to add quotes inside your strings.

Chapter Summary

This chapter was a short but comprehensive lesson that covered some important but overlooked aspects of C++. The things taught in this chapter such as the newline and tab character, are crucial to creating professional looking applications, and will definitely help you spruce up your programs in your CS class. And the method to put quotes as part of a string, are also very important. And the error beep character is also quite important because it may be a good way to get the users attention or alert the user of something important.

Chapter 8: Functions

This chapter gets a little bumpy. So get your thinking caps on. Ok. A *function* is pretty much there to save time when writing code. A programmer can't possibly write thousands of lines of code, and be organized. There's just no way. But with a function, code can be divided up and instead of re-typing the code, use a one-word function instead. It's like a book in a bookshelf. What if all of the books in the shelf had no covers and they were just a big pile of papers? They would be much easier to maintain with covers binding them together. This is what a function does. It binds together large chunks of code into a neat little function. Here's an example:

```
cout << "I am a function!" << endl;
cout << "Hear me beep!" << endl;
cout << "\a" << endl;
```

Instead of typing out all that code every time I want to use it, I can just make it into a neat little function called, how about, MyFunction. The function would look like this:

```
void MyFunction()
{
        cout << "I am a function!" << endl;
        cout << "Hear me beep!" << endl;
        cout << "\a" << endl;
}
```

A function is declared kind of like a variable. In this case, the function is a type void. Other types can be used like int and string and stuff. But this previous example is using void because the function does NOT return a value. More on that later. First off, you must understand, that the *main function* is just a function, like **MyFunction**. The only difference is that the *main function* is always called first, by default. That is just how C++ was made. C++ was made so that the *main function* will always be the first function to be called. All functions use this format:

```
<Return type> <name> ( <arguments> )
{
        <functions code goes here>
        return <what to return>;
}
```

The following example will use a very simple function:

```cpp
#include <iostream>
using namespace std;

void MyFunction();

int main()
{

        MyFunction();

        return 0;
}

void MyFunction()
{
        cout << "I am a function!" << endl;
        cout << "Hear me beep!" << endl;
        cout << "\a" << endl;
}
```

When compiled, it looks like this:

```
        I am a function!
        Hear me beep!
        <BEEP>
```

Ok. Study this example for a minute. Notice how **MyFunction** is declared after the *main function*. Remember, the function shouldn't be defined inside the *main function*. Also, notice how **void MyFunction();** is declared before the include statements at the way top. This has to be done because you must let your program know that you are making a new function. Notice how there are ( ) parenthesis after **MyFunction**. Those are meant for arguments. Arguments are variables that the function takes as input. This is called *passing* a value to a function. When you call a function and pass it a variable, the function must return a variable. Then the *main function* can use that variable. Make sure you know the format of the previous example.

Make sure you know that the function is defined OUTSIDE the *main function*, and note that the function is declared at the beginning before the *main function*. Also, make sure you know how to call the function.

The next section will explain a function with arguments and a return value.

return

There is a built-in function in C++ called *sqrt*. This function *returns* the square root of whatever value you pass to it. So if you wanted to pass the number 49 to sqrt, it would look like this:

```
int z;
z=sqrt( 49 );
```

When sqrt is passed 49, it *returns* the square root of it. And the number returned, which is 7, is assigned to z; because **z=sqrt (49)**. Get it? Easy right? It work's the same way when you make your OWN functions that return a value. For our example, let's make a function that multiplies the number passed to it, by 2. The function will be called TimesTwo. So **TimesTwo (4)** would return 8. Look:

```cpp
#include <iostream>
using namespace std;

int TimesTwo ( int nInput ); // function declared

int main()
{
      int z;
      z = TimesTwo(4);
      cout << z;

      return 0;
}

int TimesTwo ( int nInput )
{
      return nInput * 2;
}
```

First, look at the usual function format. See how the function is defined outside the *main function*? Good.

Look at the definition of the TimesTwo function. This comes after the *main function*. The line starts off with **int TimesTwo (int nInput)**. The function is a type int because it returns an int. The name of the function is **TimesTwo**. There only one argument for the function. The argument is an int, called **nInput**. **nInput** represents nothing more than an integer. It corresponds to whatever is passed to the function. The **TimesTwo** function just uses **nInput**, as if it was the value passed to it. Then the function returns it. So when you pass the number 4 to **TimesTwo**, then **TimesTwo** sees **nInput** as a 4. Get it?

Returning Functions with Multiple arguments

In the previous section, only ONE value was passed to the **TimesTwo** function. But in some cases, you may want to pass more than one value to the function. To do this, you would write the function like usual, but separate the arguments with commas. And when you return a value, you would return only the ones you want to return. You don't have to always return all the values passed to it. For example, if you have a function that does a math equation, the function may take several numbers as arguments, but only return the answer. The following is the example is the previous section, but revised, so that the **TimesTwo** function accepts two values instead. And instead of multiplying the input by 2, the function will take the two parameters passed to it, and multiply them together:

```cpp
#include <iostream>
using namespace std;

int TimesTwo ( int nInput, int nInput2 )

int main()
{
        int z;
        z = TimesTwo(4, 3);
        cout << z;

        return 0;
}

int TimesTwo ( int nInput, int nInput2 )
{
        return nInput * nInput2;
}
```

Look at the definition for the **TimesTwo** function. Notice that it returns **nInput * nInput2**, instead of **nInput * 2**. So after the previous example is compiled and run, it would look like this:

12

switch Statement

A *switch statement* is an easy way to keep your code organized. It's like a combination of an *if then loop* and a function. Here is the format for switch statements:

```
Switch ( <expression> )
{
        case <possibility> :
                <code>
                break;

        case <possibility> :
                <code>
                break;

        default:
                <skips here if no match>
}
```

That's it. That is how every switch statement you make should look like. Here is an example switch statement:

```cpp
int main()
{

    int nChoice;
    cout << "Enter a number between 1 and 3." << endl;
    cin >> nChoice;

    switch (nChoice)
    {
    case 1:
                cout << "You entered one!" << endl;
                break;
    case 2:
                cout << "You entered two!" << endl;
                break;
    case 3:

                cout << "You entered three!" << endl;
                break;
    default:
                cout << "Invalid choice!" << endl;

    }

    return 0;
}
```

Ok. This example makes use of the switch statement. We use cout to tell the user to enter a number between 1 and 3. There is a case statement for each of our choices; 1, 2, and 3. The program changes depending on which number (1, 2, or 3) the user picks. You may notice the **break;** statements at the end of each case statement. The **break;** in a switch statement must ALWAYS be there. Also, you may be wondering why there are no brackets after the **case**'s. This is because **break;** is there. The case statements keep reading the code until it reaches **break;**. Then they know it is the end of the case, and stop.

The **default:** part of the code tells the code, "use this if the user doesn't enter 1, 2, or 3!" For example, if the user enters 7, which is not one of the choices, the default statement is executed. Here is the output:

```
Enter a number between 1 and 3.
2 <ENTER>
You entered two!
```

Chapter Summary

This chapter was a mouth full. First, you learned the basic function. Which is a shortcut and a great example of code re-use, a MUST, for all object oriented programming languages. You then learned about the function using a return statement. The return statement simply returns something to the calling function. You also learned that functions with return values cannot be declared as a void function. They must be declared as whatever the return value is. For example, if your function was called CoolFunction, and it returns an int, your function should be declared as an int, not anything else. And you also learned about arguments, which are the variables passed to the function. You also learned about multiple arguments, which are very useful. The last thing in this chapter was the switch statement, which is a great way to write flexible code. It allows you to execute different pieces of code depending on the value of a variable. You'll be using the switch statement at least a couple times in your programs, so you should get used to it.

Chapter 9: Global Variables

This short but informative chapter will teach you about the *global variable*. The global variable is a variable that is global. If something is global, it means it is universal. All of the code you have seen so far have one thing in common; the variables are all declared inside of the functions. That is, all the variables are declared within the brackets of each function. If a variable is declared in the *main function*, it is not available for other functions to use. This is because the *main function* declared it, not any other function. But what do you do if you want a variable that EVERY function in your code can use? This is where global variables come in.

Look at the following example:

```cpp
#include <iostream>
using namespace std;
void MyFunction();
int nGlobalVariable;

int main()
{
        nGlobalVariable = 4 ;
        cout << nGlobalVariable << endl;

        return 0;
}
void MyFunction()
{
        nGlobalVariable = 5 ;
        cout << nGlobalVariable << endl;
}
```

Notice this code has a function called **MyFunction** in it. Look at the fourth line. You will notice that a int variable called **nGlobalVariable**, is declared. It is declared OUTSIDE any of the functions. Therefore, it is a *global variable*, and can be accessed by any function. You will notice that the *main function* uses **nGlobalVariable**, as does **MyFunction**.

Chapter Summary

This chapter covered the global variable. The global variable is simple. It is just a variable that can be used by any function in your code. So a global variable could be used by all the functions, as well as the *main function*. This is very useful if you want a variable for your entire program to share and use. This will definitely be used in your CS class.

Chapter 10: Arrays

The array is a very useful tool in C++ that not only saves time, but also space. An array can save hundreds of lines of code, and in some cases, make your program much more effective.

Arrays

Look at the following example of an array:

```
int nArray[ ] = { 23,53,64,83, 99};
cout << nArray[2];
```

The variable **nArray**, is an array of type int. If you wanted to make 20 int's, it would be easier to make an array instead of declaring each int separately.

First, you must learn how the array works. When we add a [ ] after the variable name, it tells the compiler, "Hey! I'm an array! Unlike a regular variable, I can hold more than one value!" So if you filled the [ ] with a number, it would correspond to a member of the array. In the previous example, **nArray**[2] corresponds to 64. You may be wondering why 64, and not 53. This is because 53 is the second member of the array. All arrays begin with 0. Not 1. So nArray[0] would correspond to 23. **nArray** [1] would correspond to 53. And so on. Also in an array, the semicolon goes AFTER the brackets. Just another rule in C++.

Oh, by the way, you can also fill the [ ] with your own number to declare how many values you want to hold, ahead of time. Like this:

int nArray[4]={ 23, 53, 64, 83, 99};

It's the programmer's choice, which method they prefer to use. Usually, this method is not as flexible as the first because it can get annoying to have to count all your values. Especially if you have 40 or 50 of them.

The Matrix Array

A matrix array is an array with 2 parts, or *dimensions,* to it. Look at the following example of a matrix array:

```
int nMatrixArray[2][3] =
{

        { 46, 93, 45 },
        { 22, 77, 30 }

};

cout << nMatrixArray[1][2] << endl;
```

Look at the previous example. A matrix array named **nMatrixArray** is declared. You will notice that **nMatrixArray** has two sets of [ ]. The first one contains a **2**, the second contains a **3**. This simply means that **nMatrixArray** is an array with **2** columns, and **3** values in each column. The output of the previous example would be:

30

Don't forget that arrays start off at 0, and not 1. So the [**1**] in **nMatrixArray**[**1**][**2**] would be the second column, and the [**2**] would mean the third value in the second column. Get it? Study the example again if you don't understand. Always remember that in an array, the first member of the array is 0, the second is 1, the third is 2, and so on.

Chapter Summary

This chapter covered the array. An array is a variable that can hold multiple values of the same type. So an int variable could hold other int values. Arrays are great for saving time and keeping your data organized. Instead of declaring 10 int, you could simply declare an int array with 10 members. Keep in mind that the array index starts at 0, not 1. The matrix array takes the regular array a step further by allowing you to create an array of values, organized in a table-like pattern. It can get confusing at times, but in certain cases, it could save you a lot of time and make your program more efficient and organized. You will definitely learn arrays in your class, so you should also know them. Arrays are an example of encapsulation, because it hides all the values and displays them only at the programmers' request. Also keep in mind that for an array, you don't always have to declare how many values you want it to contain, ahead of time. So you could use [], instead of [73], because it would be much simpler than counting all the values you want to put in it. The main reason for having an array is to save time by letting the programmer make his values into an index. It is very important, so don't forget it.

Chapter 11: Structures

When you use an array, you know that is can hold a bunch of different values. You also know that all the values have to be of the same type. You can create an array with 50 members of int's, and another array with 50 members of strings. But you cant make an array with ints AND strings. Not so flexible you say? This is where the structure comes in.

struct

When you create a structure, the keyword *struct* is used. Here is an example of a structure in action:

```cpp
#include <iostream>
using namespace std;

struct Qualities
{
      char LastName[30];
      int Age;
      double Weight;
};

int main()
{
      Qualities Bob =
      {
            "Simpson",
            45,
            185.3
      };

      Qualities John =
      {
            "Alberts",
            37,
            153.6
      };

cout << "Bob's last name is "<< Bob.LastName << endl;
cout << "His age is " << Bob.Age << endl;
cout << "And his weight is " << Bob.Weight << endl;
cout << endl;
cout << "John's last name is " << John.LastName << endl;
cout << "His age is " << John.Age << endl;
cout << "And his weight is " << John.Weight << endl;
```

Ok. Look over this code. Before the *main function*, that the structure is declared. The structures name is Qualities. It holds 3 members: **LastName[30]**, **Age**, and **Weight**. Now look in the *main function*. You will notice that the structure's name, **Qualities**, is used to declare a new variable called **Bob**. By preceding **Bob** with **Qualities**, you are creating an *object* of the **Qualities** structure. Also, notice that **Bob** is assigned 3 values, which correspond to what was in the structure. Bob's **LastName[30]** is assigned "Simpson". Bob's **Age** is assigned 45. And Bob's **Weight** is assigned **185.3**. By using the *membership operator (.)* you can access these values. For example, Bob.Age would be 45.

The exact same thing that was done to **Bob**, is also done to **John**. A new object of Qualities is created. It is called John. Then the members are all given values. Here is the output of the previous example:

Bob's last name is Simpson
His age is 45
And his weight is 185.3

Bob's last name is Alberts
His age is 37
And his weight is 153.6

Get it? If you don't, study the example again. You MUST understand the previous example because the next chapter will discuss *classes,* which are extremely similar to structures.

Chapter Summary

The structure is a "simple class." That will be discussed in the next chapter, but for now, just remember that the structure is created using the keyword **struct**. It is a great form of code-reuse and the structure accesses it's members by using the *membership operator (.).* The next chapter will cover classes, which make structures obsolete. But you should always learn structures before classes, because they are so similar and go together nicely. You will almost definitely be taught structures in your class, so you should have a good understanding of them.

Chapter 12: Classes

Ok. This is probably going to be the hardest part of this book, so pay close attention. The heart of OOP is based on the ability of C++ to create and maintain *classes*. In the previous chapter, you learned structures. Classes, as I mentioned earlier, are extremely similar to classes.

The Class

Classes, in a way, are more complex structures. I'll show you what I mean. Look at the format for a class:

```
class <name>
{
public:
  <public members>

};
```

In the **public** members area, you put variables and functions. Variables define in a class are called member variables, and functions defined in a class are member functions. Some people like to call member functions *methods,* but this won't be used in this book. And probably not in your computer science course either, for that matter.

Here is an example of a simple class in action:

```cpp
#include <iostream>
using namespace std;

class Blah // class is defined
{

public:
 int nMember;
 int TimesTwo(int nInput)
    {
       return nInput * 2;
    }

};

int main()
{
       Blah NewObject; // New object created
       int x = NewObject.TimesTwo(3); // Uses . to access member
                              // function

       cout << x << endl;

       return 0;
}
```

First off, notice the class being declared before the *main function*. It uses the same format as the one given before. You may notice that the class definition is similar to that of a structure. Except that the class has all of it's member variables and functions listed under **public:**. The **public:** statement means that all of the member variables and functions listed under it, can be accessed from anywhere.

You can also have *private,* and *protected,* instead of public. Or, you can have all three. Whatever you want. If the members are private, that means that they can only be accessed from other members of the same class. And for protected members, the members are available in the same way as a private, but also to derived classes. These will all be covered later.

Back to the example. Notice that an object of class **Blah** is created, called **NewObject**. This is done in the line:

Blah NewObject;

Just like in a structure, the *membership operator (.)* is used to access the public members of the class. Like so:

int x=NewObject.TimesTwo(4);

Also, look at the class definition. See how the code for the **TimesTwo** function is defined *INSIDE* the class? Well, it doesn't have to be declared there. If you want to make your class look more simple then you can adjust the previous example like so:

```
class Blah
{
public:
 int nMember;
 int TimesTwo(int nInput); // function NOT defined
                           // inside class
};

Blah::TimesTwo (int nInput) // function defined here instead
{
        return nInput * 2;
}
```

Here you see, for the first time, the *scope resolution operator (::).*
It is placed in between the class name and the function you want
to define. Then you just simply define the function like any other.

Why Classes?

Right now, you may be wondering why classes are necessary
if you can just use a structure instead. That is because of the
class's ability to create public, private, or protected members.
This is very important to the concept of hiding data, a huge part
of OOP. Also, classes are a form of cod re-use. Another big thing
in OOP. This allows you to write functions and variables ahead
of time and use them over and over with the help of the

membership operator (.). Basically, classes ARE structures, with some extra advantages. For you computer science course, classes will probably be the one thing that the rest of your class will have trouble on. It is a hard concept to understand.

Derived Classes

Deriving a class from another class is a form of code re-use. Deriving a class is called *class inheritance*, because the derived class INHERITS members from the class it was derived from. An example should clear this up.

Your house represents a class. And the stuff inside your house represents the members of the class. You don't want a stranger to have access to the stuff in your house, so you have a lock on the door. And only the people that have the key can have access to the stuff in your house.

Deriving a class from another class is like giving the class a key to your house. Let's say you have a class called **House**. And another class called **Person**. If you derive **Person** from **House**, then **Person** will have the key to **House**, and can access all of **House's** public and protected members, or stuff. Get it? But **Person** still can't access the **private** members. But don't worry about that for now. It will be explained later.

When you derive a class, the original class is called the *base class*. And the class that is derived from the base class is called the *derived class*. You would use the : operator to derive a class. Here is an example:

class DerivedClass: public BaseClass

In the following example, **DerivedClass** is derived from **BaseClass**. Which means that **DerivedClass** inherits members from **BaseClass**. This example should explain:

```
#include <iostream>
using namespace std;

class BaseClass
{
public:
 int member;
};

class DerivedClass : public BaseClass
{
     ...
};

int main()
{
     DerivedClass NewObject;
     NewObject.member = 3;
     return 0;
}
```

See how **DerivedClass** gains access to **BaseClass?** This is class inheritance! Anyways, next we will learn about the *constructor* and *destructor* of a class.

Constructor and Destructor

The *constructor* of a class is a function that has the exact same name as the class name. So if the class is named Blah, the constructor would be called Blah. The constructor is the function that is usually used to set values to variables when an object is created. When the class object is created, the constructor is run automatically. Likely, the *destructor* is a function that is automatically run when an object is destroyed. When the code block where the class object is used is exited, or no longer used, the destructor is called. Also, when you delete a class object after it has been created with *new*, the destructor is run. Don't worry about the new and delete thing until the next chapter. Likewise, the destructor also has the same name as the class, but is always begun with a ~ sign. Look at the following example, which makes use of the destructor and constructor:

```cpp
#include <iostream>
using namespace std;

class Blah
{
public:
  Blah();
 ~Blah();

};

Blah::Blah()
{
      cout << "Constructing!" << endl;
}

Blah::~Blah()
{
      cout << "Destructing!" << endl;
}

int main()
{
      Blah NewObject;
      return 0;
}
```

When the **Blah** class creates a new object called **NewObject**, it automatically calls the constructor, because **NewObject** is being constructed, or created. And when the program exits, **NewObject** is being destroyed, or destructed. So it calls the destructor. The output is:

Constructing!
Destructing!

Chapter Summary

This chapter may have been a bit overwhelming. It covered a huge amount of OOP and C++. Classes are simply a more advanced *structure*, so you should have no trouble understanding classes, if you are already familiar with the *structure*. Keep in mind that classes are the heart of C++ and the main reason why it is chosen over so many other programming languages. It demonstrates not only code re-use, but also encapsulation and flexibility of C++. Classes will keep your code organized and easy to read. Remember that classes are probably going to be the thing that students have the most trouble with, so make sure you have a good understanding of classes. This chapter covered about 80% of classes, which is everything you need to know.

Chapter 13: Pointers and Memory Allocation

Pointers are a way in C++ to save memory and make good use of memory allocation. When you create a variable or an object, it takes up some, not a lot, but some space on your computer. That is, it takes up some memory. This is ok because they don't take up a lot of space. For example, an int only takes up 4 bytes. But when programs become very large, it can pose the threat of using up TOO much memory and corrupting data, or even worse, crashing your program. Pointers are what make C++ different from so many other languages. Even Java, which is so similar to C++ that only a competent C++ programmer can tell them apart, doesn't use pointers. That shows how significant the pointer is to C++. This chapter is focused at teaching you how, when, and why to use pointers. Let's begin.

Memory and C++

Your computer is filled with memory. And this memory is located in *memory addresses*. Let's say you have a chunk of land about 10 miles long and 10 miles wide. And every time you create a new variable or object, a new house is built. This obviously takes up space. Not a lot, but still takes up some space. So instead of building a new house every time you create something, *pointers* allow you to "point" to a piece of land and say, "that is where the new house is going to be." That is all it does, but doesn't actually build the house.

Pointers do this by allowing you to "point" to a space in memory, or memory addresses. This memory address then represents an object or variable you created. And by combining this with the *delete* operator, you can even delete the memory addresses after you are through using them. But that will be discussed a little later.

Pointers are created by using the * operator. Yes, it is the same as the multiplication sign, but it is used in a different way. Here is how you allocate a memory address for an int:

int * nInteger;

This allocates space for an int in memory. In order to declare a pointer, just place a * in between the variable type and name being declared.

Another interesting thing about pointers is that it can be done also, with classes. You can create a pointer to a class object. So if you had a class named NewClass, you could create a pointer to a NewClass object like so:

NewClass * NewObject;

But when you use a pointer to create an object, instead of using the *membership operator (.)* to access it's members, you use the *pointer membership operator (->)*. It looks like an arrow, but it's just a hyphen and a greater than sign put together.

In C++, the **&** sign means "address of." So **&nInteger** would mean the address of **nInteger**. Look at this example:

```
int nInteger;
int * nInteger2;

nInteger2 = &nInteger;
*nInteger2 = 5;

cout << nInteger << endl;
cout << *nInteger2 << endl;
```

Look at the line that says **nInteger2=&nInteger;**. You will see that **nInteger2** now points to **nInteger**. Then at the line *nInteger2=5, it stores 5 into a memory address, and since **nInteger2=&nInteger**, they both point to the same address, and both equal 5. The output is:

5

5

Pointers can also be passed to functions like any other variable or object. Look at this self-explanatory example of pointers being passed to a function named TimesTwo:

```cpp
#include <iostream>
using namespace std;

int TimesTwo(int ninput);


int main()
{

        int *v;
        *v = 4;
        TimesTwo(*v);

        return 0;

}




int TimesTwo(int ninput)
{
        return ninput * 2;
}
```

The output is:

8

new and delete

C++, as you have noticed, is a very flexible language, that allows the programmer to be in charge as much as possible. The *new* and *delete* operators take this to the next level by allowing the programmer to specifically create and delete their own memory. The *new* and *delete* operators are used with pointers to allocate memory. These operators allow your program to create and delete memory spaces DURING program execution. By using the *new* operator to create a new space in memory for whatever is being declared, and then using *delete*, to delete it, allows the user to manage memory in their program. It's like using pointers, except YOU get to decide when and how it will be deleted and created. Oh, and when you declare pointers, we proceed the name with the letter *"p"*. Kind of like how we proceed int with *"n"* and string with *"sz."* This technique will be carried out from this point of the book. Anyways, look at this example:

```cpp
#include <iostream>
using namespace std;


int main()
{

        int * pInteger = new int; // use new to
                        //allocate new memory
        *pInteger = 5;
        cout << *pInteger;

        delete pInteger; //use delete to delete
                                //this memory
        return 0;


}
```

Look at the first line inside the *main function*. You will notice that the pointer, **pInteger**, is declared like a normal pointer, except at the end,=**new int**, is added. This is the format for using the *new* operator. Then at the second to last line of the *main function*, you see *delete* being used to delete **pIntegers** from memory. It is ok in this case to delete **pInteger** because we are through using it. But don't ever delete a pointer until it is no longer needed. For example, if you created a variable with *new,* then deleted it, and some other function needed to use it, your program would error. So always double check to make sure nothing is dependant on your pointer before you delete it.

Another important issue of the *new and delete* operators is the *memory leak*. A memory leak can occur in your program if you create a variable with *new*, and don't ever delete it with *delete*. Remember that the *new* operator saves space in memory for you, and if you don't delete it, your program will keep holding onto that space of memory, and causes memory leaks. Even just a few memory leaks are bad because they give your program a good chance of crashing or losing data. And especially when your program gets really big, memory leaks get harder and harder to find, and can do even more damage. Don't forget to delete anything you create, it's VERY IMPORTANT!

Array Pointers

Arrays can also be declared as pointers, the exact same way as any other pointer would be. But instead of using *new* and *delete*, we use *new[]* and *delete[]*.

Chapter Summary

This chapter taught you how to manage memory in your programs by using pointers to "point" to a space in memory, instead of consume that space for a variable. You also learned about the *new* and *delete* operators, which leave it up to the programmer to locate and delete memory addresses. Remember that you should never delete a pointer unless you are sure that the rest of your code no longer relies on it. Don't delete a pointer, if later in your code, a function tries to use that pointer. It will cause errors which could have easily have been avoided. You may or may not learn pointers in your class, depending on your teachers pace. But even if you don't learn it, you should always have a knowledge of pointers because they are very important and used all the time in C++ programming. But chances are, you will learn pointers in your class.

Chapter 14: const, Namespace, and the ? Operator

Compiling Separately

As mentioned earlier, compilers are the programs that make your C++ code into a program. When C++ code gets too long, programmers like to separate their files. They are still part of the same *project*, but of different files. For example, if you wrote a class that is 33 pages long, and you wrote a function that is 30 pages long, you probably wouldn't want to have them all in one file, because it would be so complicated to manage.

Also, when you use more than one file, they are usually .cpp or .h. Remember, .h is a header, and .cpp is a C++ file. Header files usually contain information that come before the *main functions*. Such as class definition, global variables, definitions of other functions, or whatever you want. You can even have the *main function* be in a file of it's own. It doesn't matter. But make sure that when you do this, you put **#include "filename"** in the include directives. This is just like putting **#include <iostream>**, except that you are using your *own* file name. And when you are using your *own* file, you must always have *quotes* around the filename, instead of < > signs.

Don't be thinking it's a hard thing to do. When you compile, the compiler compiles ALL of the smaller files instead of just one big one, as long as the include directives are all in there. Otherwise, the compiler wouldn't know what to do. That's all there is to it. Don't worry, this is not a big deal in C++, and plus, you will be taught how to do it in your class, since not all compilers do this the same way. So you don't really need to be worried about it for now.

using namespace std;

In all of the examples in this book, the phrase **using namespace std;** seems to appear at the beginning of every file. When you insert include directives, you are including functions and operators that are in the predefined header file you are using. For example, cin and cout are part of the predefined header file, iostream.h. So by including the namespace definition at the beginning of the file, you are sparing yourself the time of having to use std::cout, std::cin, or anything like that. Instead, you just put cout and cin. This book won't go any further into namespaces. They aren't really that important, especially in your computer science class. But it's always good to know why the namespace definition is there.

? Conditional Operator

The *? operator* is a shortcut to the *if else* statement. It's actually pretty simple. It's merely an *if then* statement, simplified drastically. Here is the format of the *? operator*:

Expression1 **?** *expression2*: *expression3*

If *expression1* is TRUE, then the value is equal to *expression2*, and if it is false, is it equal to *expression3*. So for example, if you had the statement: **9 > 4 ? 1: 0**, since **9 > 4** is true, the value of the statement would be **1**. Likewise, if the expression were **4 > 9: 1 ? 0**, the value of the statement would be 0 because **4 > 9** is false.

You don't need to see this operator in action because you already know how to use the *if else statement*. Also, this even may or may not be covered in your course. But like usually, it's always better safe than sorry.

const variables

If you ever want to create a variable that CAN'T ever change, you precede the entire declaration with *const*. For example, **const int nInteger=30;** would create an **int** named **nInteger**, that has a constant and unchangeable value of **30**. So if you put **const int nInteger=30;** as a global in your program, you could use the word **nInteger** instead of **30** for the rest of the program! Pretty neat huh?

You may be wondering why this is necessary. We can just create a regular non-constant variable and store the data in it. Can't we? The answer is yes we can. But if we do this, it wouldn't be very effective because the data could be changed at any time. For example, let's say you put **int ten=10;** as a global. From then on, you can use **ten** instead of **10**. But since this isn't a constant variable, the data, which is 10, could get corrupted. Especially if your program is larger and that variable is used a lot. Computers can be very random and do weird things, so you never know what can happen to your variable. It is always safer to use *const* when you don't want your variable's value changed. Always.

Chapter Summary

This chapter was pretty straight forward and covered a variety of topics. Compiling your files separately saves time, and keeps your code more organized, especially for your larger projects. And the namepspace is usually declared to save time, as is the ? operator, if you don't want or need to write an *if then* statement. The keyword *const* is used to set a variables value as permanent. So a const int that has a value of 10, will always be 10, and won't ever be changed. When a global const is declared, it is usually done because the programmer doesn't want to re-write the value over and over. For example, if your program heavily relied on the number 7,324,950 and you didn't want to re-write that number every time you needed to use it, you could just create a const global variable named nImportant with the value of 7,324,950 and use that instead. You will probably learn all of the topics covered in this chapter, except for maybe the namespace. But keep them in mind as always, because you never know when you might need it.

Chapter 15: Strategies in Comp Sci

In Computer Science, most of your work, if not all, will revolve around writing your own code to solve problems or do specific tasks that the teacher assigns you. Even if you know C++ and how to program, it won't help much unless you know how to develop solutions for the tasks. A lot of your assignments will probably deal with things like math problems and user input. This chapter is dedicated to teaching you how to create programs from questions given to you as assignments. You will learn strategies on developing solutions and writing code to solve problems and do tasks. Let's begin.

Knowing Your Language

In your comp sci class, your assignments will not be bombarded together. They will be given out, and the assignments will cover subject matter already taught to you in that class. For example, if you were taught a section on variables, most likely, your next assignment or test will ask you to make a program using variables or something. Everything you need to know is probably going to be taught to you. But what makes writing code so hard is the fact that you have to combine all your knowledge together to solve the problem assigned to you. The best advice I can give is that you must know your programming language. You must know C++. You can't write a good speech if you can barely speak English. You can't write a good program in C++ if you don't understand C++. Make sure that you use this book, and read ahead of time the things you will be taught in your class. Then when it comes along, you can zip through it because you already know it!

Math Problems

In all you assignments, there will always be some sort of problem. Remember, every code you write is written to solve a problem. Whenever you are given an assignment in your class, the first thing you should always do is identify the problem. For example, if your homework assignment was to write code that solves a math problem, identify the problem first. In this case, the problem is a type of math problem. Look at it and work the problem out. Then apply it to C++ and write it out in code. This may seem harder than it sounds at some times.

For example, you may be given a problem that asks you to add 30 to whatever number the user inputs, and then display it onto the screen. This is easy right? The problem here is adding 30 to the user's input and finding the answer. Let's work this out like a math problem and let X represent the number that the user inputs. X + 30=answer! You have just found the solution to the problem! The solution is X + 30. Now you want to translate this into code. First off, look at what the assignment is asking you to do. The assignment is asking you to get the user input, add 30, and display it. Now think about C++ and how you could do this. You could create a variable to represent the user input and use cin to get it. Then you can use the math operators to solve the problem and use cout to display it.

Here is a summary of the steps I took to solve the problem and write the code. First, I identify the problem. Second, I find the solution to that problem. And third, I apply the solution to C++ and create the code, using the solution to solve the problem. Even for bigger and more complex assignments, if they require math, chances are you can apply this technique to it.

Subject Matter Problems

Some of the programs you make in your comp sci class may require that you write code that uses what you have just learned. For example, let's say that you're in comp sci class, and you just learned about arrays. The teacher may ask you to write code that uses arrays and shows them in action. This is simple. We have been doing this throughout this entire book and it is not so hard. It just applies basic principles to code to show a certain point. That is, if we're asked to use an array, we can just create a program that sets values to an array of int's and then displays them onto the screen, or something simple like that.

When you do these kinds of problems, think "simple." Unless your told otherwise, if the teacher gives you a simple assignment to show how variables are used, don't write 20 pages of code that gets the percent increase of a variable and adds it to the memory address of a pointer value of a string. Why would you need all that? The assignment asks you to use a variable. Not all that other stuff.

Bigger Programs

Most assignments in comp sci usually fall into the two categories mentioned previously. Sometimes, though, you may be asked to create a bigger program for a test or maybe even for your final exam. They are similar to regular, smaller programs, except that bigger programs would require more code, which would lead to more complex code. Don't worry about this. This is something that only practice would help you. And since your comp sci class will start small and work up to bigger programs, you shouldn't have too much trouble on them. It is just good to know what to expect in your course.

Putting It All Together

Ok. This section will be giving you five practice problems. The first, we will do together, and I want you to try the last four on your own. You can use any C++ compiler (if you don't have one, just go on the web and look up search phrases like *"C++ Compiler Free"* or *"C++ compiler download."*) But it's ok if you don't have one. You can still try applying some of the things we discussed in this chapter to the practice problems. Try identifying the problems, finding solutions, and think about what you would do to apply the solution to code. You can even make an outline or take notes about the problem, if it will help you. Feel free to flip through this book if you need any help.

Practice Problem 1

ABCD Banks Inc. charges 8% of how much you borrow from them, as a fee.

You have just been hired to create a program that does this. The programs allows the user to enter in how much money they want to borrow, maximum $4000, and then displays how much the fee will be. Create this program.

Ok. First, let's identify the problem they you must solve. The program allows the user to enter in how much they would like to borrow. And then displays the fee, which is 8%. That is the problem right there. You want to be able to display 8% of whatever the user inputs. So to solve that problem, your solution could be several things. But the best one is to use the percent formula, which you should have learned in geometry. That is, to find 8% of, let's say, X, you would multiply X by .08. So if the user types in 100, and you multiply that by .08, you would get 8. You also want to remember that the MAXIMUM amount the user can borrow is $4000.

You also want to keep in mind that these assignments should look and be as professional as possible. Pretend you really ARE hired by ABCD Banks. Make the program look good. Here is the code you can use to solve the assignment:

```cpp
#include <iostream>
using namespace std;
const int Thirty = 30;
void BorrowMoney ();

int main()
{
    cout << "\t\t\tABCD Banks Inc." << endl;
    cout << "\t\t\t_____" << endl;
    cout << endl << endl;
    //Title to make program look more professional
BorrowMoney();
    return 0;
}

void BorrowMoney ()
{
    char cName[Thirty];
    int nBorrow;

    cout << "Enter your name: " << endl;
    cin >> cName;

    cout << endl << endl; //spacing to make it look good
    cout << "How much would you like to borrow, "
        << cName << "?" << endl;
    cin >> nBorrow;
    if (nBorrow > 4000)
    {
        cout << "You cannot borrow more than $4000." << endl;
        cout << endl << endl << endl;
        BorrowMoney();
    }

else
    {
    cout << endl << endl; //spacing to make it look good
        cout << "You have chosen to borrow $" << nBorrow <<
            " . Your fee is $" << 0.08 * nBorrow <<
            "." << endl;
    cout << "Thank you for choosing ABCD Banks Inc." << endl;
    }
    return;
```

This code makes good use of a lot of the features in C++. Your teacher will like that. Read over the code and identify all the methods we used to create this program.

First, we simply use cout with some *tab characters* (\t) to make a fancy looking title, to give the program a more professional look. Then, we simply call the function, **BorrowMoney**(). This function uses cout and cin to ask the user questions and get their input. The user inputs their name and the amount they want to borrow. Immediately after the user types in the amount they want to borrow, an *if else loop* checks to see if the amount typed in is greater than 4000. Remember, the assignment said that the user cannot borrow more than $4000. So if the input is over 4000, we simply use cout to notify the user that the amount is too large. Then we simply call **BorrowMoney**() function again to let the user start over, and re-type everything. When the user inputs a value less than 4000, we use a simple math formula to find 8% of the input, and display it on the screen. Not too hard; you might want to try the following practice problems if you have access to a C++ compiler. Here is the output, showing the outcome of typing a number greater than 4000, and less than 4000:

ABCD Banks Inc.

_____

Enter your name:
Sam<ENTER>

How much would you like to borrow, Sam?
9000000000<ENTER>
You cannot borrow more than $4000.

Enter your name:
Sam

How much would you like to borrow, Sam?
350<ENTER>

You have chosen to borrow $350. Your fee is $28.
Thank you for choosing ABCD Banks Inc.

Practice Problems

Try the rest of these practice questions on your own. They are arranged in order of difficulty. If you don't have access to a compiler, try identifying problems and try associating C++ code to these problems instead.

Create a program that simply shows the use of a nested loop. It should be simple and clear. Create this program.

Create a program that counts to 100, then beeps to let the user know that it has finished.

A trading company has asked you to create a program that will allow the user to input 5 names. Each of these names will be inputted into an array and then displayed onto the screen at the user's request. Create this program.

Zorfinbab Inc. has hired you to create a program to organize ID numbers for employees. Create a program using classes and member functions, which allows the user to type in a user name, and then have a number appear for each different ID. For example, if the user types in Bob as the first ID number, the response is 1. Then the next ID would be 2, 3, 4, and so on. Create this program.

Chapter Summary

This chapter was dedicated to the computer science student, and gave tips on creating and solving your assignments. A huge chunk of your CS class will be given to write code and create programs. And your homework may be to write code that solves problems, like the ones listed previously. Remember that practice makes perfect, and creating your own programs is a great way to learn. You should always find the solution to the problem before writing any code. When you solve the main problem, it is called the *design phase* of your program. Don't worry about that term for right now, it probably won't even come up in your class.

Chapter 16: Debugging

In computer science, as well as every day programming, the most common thing that will stop a programmer from writing a good program are *bugs*. A bug is something in your code that causes it to have errors or not to work properly, if at all. There is no way around a bug, unless you're the perfect programmer, whom still can't ALWAYS avoid bugs.

It's like typing a twenty-page research paper. Obviously, your going to miss commas, misspell a word, or whatever. Chances are, you won't write your paper perfectly without any errors, the first time you type it up. The same goes for C++. If you leave something out, forget to capitalize something, whatever the error may be, it will cause a bug in your code. Most compilers have a *debugging* feature. The compiler at your computer science course will almost definitely have one. It is not what it sounds like though. It does not actually debug the program for you. Instead, if simply finds the error and reports them to you, so you may fix them. The errors, as mentioned earlier, are displayed in the *debug window,* and the line number where the error occurred is usually also displayed. But don't always trust the line number. Sometimes, errors may be RELATED to the line, or maybe a couple up or down from it. It's your knowledge of C++ that will help you solve bugs.

Bugs are, without a doubt, the biggest reason why programming is so difficult. The errors are inevitable, in any programming language. Especially in C++, there are several rules and regulations you must follow when programming. If you misspell or leave out any syntax, you will have a bug. The best way to avoid bugs are to catch them ahead of time, while your writing the code. If not, you can always go back and fix them later. Remember, practice makes perfect. Especially in debugging code.

Commenting Your Code

One of the most important things about keeping your code bug-free is using the comments. When your writing code, who knows how long and complex it can get? You need comments to organize everything. Not literally everything, but enough to guide you through your code without getting lost. Just write short little comments while you are writing the code. It will be much easier to read once you are finished with it, or if there is ever the need to modify or change the code. There's nothing more frustrating than getting lost in C++ code, especially when that code was written by you.

Warnings

Accompanying your bugs are warnings. Warnings are mentioned by your compiler when you compile, but do not stop you from compiling your code. Remember that a bug in your code is an error and will not allow you to compile your code. Having warning, however, will still allow you to compile the code, but your program may experience defects and unexpected errors. That is why a warning should never be ignored. The warning will also give you a description of what is wrong and where it is wrong. Ignoring warnings can only cause harm to your program, so make sure you fix warnings. If you don't know what a warning means, look it up. There are too many of them to explain.

Careless Mistakes

A lot of times, even the most advanced programmer, may make careless mistakes in their code. They might misspell a word or forget a ; or whatever. If you are ever stuck trying to debug a program, before you do anything, look for the careless mistakes. Look for missing ; or {} or (). Look for misspelled keywords. Who knows? Maybe you misspelled *switch*, or *int*, or *void*. A lot of the times, students find themselves wasting valuable time trying to find the error in their code, when all along, it was right in front of their face. Don't waste time doing this; as soon as the compiler finds an error, look for careless mistakes first, before you try to re-arrange the code or try anything else.

Memory Leaks

Memory leaks cannot be stressed enough in a program. Make sure your program is totally free of memory leaks. Some compilers may warn the user of memory leaks, but users will do little, if anything, to try to fix it. Memory leaks are very hard to track down, especially when programs get longer and larger. Make sure you keep track of all the objects you create with *new,* even write them down, so that you won't forget to delete them later, and spare yourself the hassle of having to track down the leak.

Chapter Summary

The main reason why it takes so long to write code is because of bugs. As long as there are computer languages, there will always be bugs. Debugging code can be time consuming and mind wrecking. Avoid this by looking for careless and simple mistakes first, before moving onto bigger things. Although code that is filled with warnings can still compile, you should always try to avoid warnings in your programs. Even though they don't affect the compile, they will almost certainly cause errors when your program is run. You will probably not learn any specific ways to debug code in your CS class, because it is not part of the C++ language. So use this chapter as a guide, and if you learn any new techniques, write them down, and try applying them to your other programs.

Glossary

This is a collection of vocabulary that is used in C++. Some of them, you may learn, and some you may not. Some of these words are not covered in this book, but they are included in case you may ever need them in the future. Perhaps in computer science C++ AP.

!—Not TRUE, makes something false.

!=—Does not equal.

*—Multiply operator. Also declares pointers.

;—Signals end of code.

+, -—addition and subtraction operators.

%—Find remainder of number.

//, */—Comments.

++—Increment.

——Decrement

=—Assignment Operator.

==—Comparison Operator.

.—Membership Operator

->—Membership Operator to a pointer.

&&—AND logical operator.

||—OR

abstract class—A class that has at least one or more pure virtual functions.

access control—refers to something that gives access to only certain parts of the code. An example of access control would be the members of a class, either they be public, private, or protected.

aggregate—Initialize

allocation—Giving memory space to an object. Like using new and delete keywords.

analysis phase—The phase when working on a project, that the problem and solution is analyzed and solved.

ANSI—American National Standards Institute. Gives programming standards and rules to the C++ programming language.

argument—Refers to the values passed to the function.

argument matching—Form of polymorphism

array—An index of values passed to a single declaration of a variable.

asm—Assembly Language. Also a keyword in C++, not used as much.

assignment—To assign a value to an existing object.

base class—Derived classes derive from this.

bool—C++ keyword used to declare a Boolean data type. Can only be assigned TRUE, FALSE, or 1, 0.

break—A C++ keyword commonly used in a switch statement, to signal the end of a code fragment, and breaks out of the code fragment.

C—Older version of C++. Different programming languages.

case—Defines the elements that a switch statement can use.

cast—The process of changing a data type into another. Type-cast.

catch—Declares an exception handler.

char—A keyword to declare a data type that can be assigned one character.

cin—Member of iostream.h, used to input data from the user.

class—Keyword to declare a class. Class is a collection of member variables and function. Members are accessed by objects and the membership operator (.).

class hierarchy—A.k.a. base class.

class library—Set of classes declared in include statements.

class member—Member of a class. Public, private, or protected.

class template—Template that is used in generating class types.

coding phase—Phase of a project where the problem and solution are applied to C++ code.

comments—Side notes included in code, uses /* and */, or //.

compiler—A program that converts C++ into assembly language. Compilers for almost every language available.

const—Keyword to declare a constant data type.

constructor—Member function of a class, with the same name as the class. Automatically called whenever a class object is declared.

conversion—Converting a data type to another type.

copy constructor—Called by a class when object is copied. A special form of a constructor.

cout—Member of iostream.h, used to display data onto the screen.

deallocation—Opposite of allocation. Deletes memory space.

debugger—Tool, common tool with most compilers, that find errors and bugs in code, and reports them.

declaration—Used to introduce something into the code.

delete operator—Keyword used to *delete* a pointer allocated with *new*.

delete[] operator—Same as the *delete* operator, but for deleting arrays.

demotion—When data is converted, its value might change. For example, converting a a float of 1.1 to an int would demote the value to 1.

derived class—The class that inherits members from a base class.

destructor—Opposite of the constructor. Same name as the class name but first character is always a ~ sign. Is automatically called when the object is destroyed.

dialect—Style of programming.

do—Same as the *while* loop.

double—Keyword to declare a larger float type.

dynamic storage—Refers to creating and deleting memory during program execution, with the new and delete operators.

dynamic_cast—Style of cast used with run-time type information available.

early-binding—Non-Polymorphic.

else—Keyword; part of the *if else* loop.

encapsulation—Concept of Object Oriented Programming. Means to hide or enclose data.

enum—Declares an enumeration. Keyword.

enumerator—Member of an enumeration.

exception—Value of a thrown type.

exception handler—Part of code that catches the exception.

exception handling—Process in which an exception has occurred in the program and handling it to do a certain task.

explicit—Indicates to constructor that it cannot declare an initializer.

expression—Combination of constants, variables, and operators that is used to create a certain value.

expression statement—example: function.

extern—Keyword to declare external name.

external name—See global variable.

false—Value of a Boolean (bool) value

float—A keyword to declare floating type.

for—Looping keyword.

friend—Keyword to give other classes and functions access to its members.

function—Combines code, arguments, and a return value to create a package of code that can be delivered by using the functions name, accompanied by arguments.

garbage collection—Automatically deleting allocated memory. C++ does not have garbage collection built in, thus the *new* and *delete* operators must be used by the programmer.

global name—A name declared so that any function can use it.

global namespace—Namespace where global variables are stored.

global variable—Variable that can be accessed by any part of the program.

goto—Keyword, transfers control within a function.

header—Header file.

header file—Copied into program using include directives. Defines sets of functions and classes for use in the program.

if—Keyword used in an *if then* loop.

inheritance—Process of a derived class inheriting members from its base class.

initialization—To assign an object a value.

inline—Keyword to create an inline function.

inline function—A function that is expanded when it is called, to save time.

int—Keyword to declare an integer.

keyword—Built in code for C++. Used to create or do basic tasks. Examples are int, string, void, for, switch, etc.

label—Name of the target of a goto statement.

linker—Produces an executable program using code. Example is a C++ compiler.

local variable—Variable declared locally in a function.

long—Declares a long integer type.

member—Class member.

member function—A function that is a member of a class.

method—Another name for a member function.

multiple inheritance—Derived class with multiple base classes.

name space—The grouping of names in a program.

namespace—Keyword used to declare a name space.

nested class—A class declared inside anther class.

new operator—Keyword used to create space in memory for an object. Should be accompanied with the *delete* character.

new[] operator—The new operator used for arrays.

object—Refers to the instance of a class. Can also be referred to as variables or data types.

object-oriented—Type of programming that emphasizes the use of encapsulation, polymorphism, and code re-use.

OOP—Object-oriented programming.

parameter—Variables passed to a function.

pointer—Address of an object.

polymorphism—Ability to change and determine the outcome of an execution. Concept of OOP.

problem—Programming is done to solve this.

private—Keyword that is used to declare that a class member can be accessed only
by member functions and friends of that class.

protected—Declares that a class member can only be accessible to it's member functions and friends of it's own class, and by members functions and friends of a derived class.

public—Declares that members of it's class can be accessible from anywhere.

pure virtual function—A virtual function with an ititializer of "=0"

reference—A.k.a. object.

return—Keyword to return values from a function.

return value—Value returned from a function using the *return* keyword.

RTTI—A.k.a. Run-time Type Information.

scope—Where a name is visible.

short—Keyword to declare small integers.

signed—Keyword used to declare signed data types.

sizeof—Keyword used to find the size of an object or data type.

solution—Main goal of programming.

statement—The part of the program that does the main work.

static object—Unchanging object.

string—Keyword to declare a string of text.

struct—Keyword to declare a structure.

switch—Keyword for declaring a switch statement.

syntax—C++ grammar.

tag—Name of a class, union, or a structure.

this—Points to the object that is being operated on. Can only be used from the member function of a class.

throw—Keyword to initiate an exception.

true—Value type for Boolean values.

unsigned—Declares unsigned type.

variable—An object that is declared, and can have value(s) assigned to it.

vector—One-dimensional array.

void—Keyword to declare no type.

while—Keyword to loop.

Index

If you need to look up something, I suggest using the table of contents, as everything in this book is organized into groups.

.cpp, 8, 91

.h, 8, 13-14, 16, 30, 32, 91-92, 114-115

? Conditional Operator, 93

Abstract Class, 112

Allocation, 83, 112, 115

ANSI, 113

arguments, 15, 19, 36, 55, 57, 62, 118

Array, 66-70, 89, 98, 104, 113, 123

Assignment, 96-99, 101-102, 112-113

B, 3, 23-25, 66

BASIC, 8, 11, 29, 36, 61, 98, 119

Bjarne Stroustrup, 3

Bool, 24, 113, 118

Brackets, 8, 15-17, 19, 41, 61, 63, 67

Break, 61, 113

Bug, 106-107

BUILD, 4, 7, 84

C, 13, 15, 17, 19, 21-24, 26-28, 30-31, 33-36, 38-39, 41, 43, 46, 48, 50-51, 53, 55, 66-67, 74, 82-83, 85, 87, 90-92, 96-99, 102-104, 106-107, 109, 111, 113-115, 118-120, 123

C++, 13, 15, 17, 19, 21-24, 26-28, 30-31, 33-36, 38-39, 41, 43, 46, 48, 50-51, 53, 55, 66-67, 74, 82-83, 85, 87, 90-92, 96-99, 102-104, 106-107, 109, 111, 113-115, 118-120, 123

Case, 7-8, 15, 36, 45, 53, 61, 88, 97, 111, 114

catch, 107, 114

Char, 24, 28, 33, 114

Cin, 30-32, 40, 46, 92, 98, 102, 114

Class, 13-14, 16, 18, 20, 24, 26-27, 31-32, 51, 65, 69, 73-80, 84, 90-92, 96-99, 104-105, 109, 112-116, 119-121, 123

Class Member Functions, 75

Class Object, 80, 84, 115

Comma Operator, 35

Commenting, 17, 107

Comparison Operator, 46, 112

Compiler, 4-7, 9-10, 13, 15, 17-19, 39, 41, 50, 66, 92, 99, 102-104, 106-108, 115, 120

Compiler, 4-7, 9-10, 13, 15, 17-19, 39, 41, 50, 66, 92, 99, 102-104, 106-108, 115, 120

Compiling Separately, 91

Const, 91, 93-95, 115

Constructor, 80, 82, 115-117

Cout, 9, 16-17, 19, 23, 25, 30-32, 40-41, 45-46, 50, 61, 92, 98, 102, 115

Deallocation, 115

Debugging, 106-107, 109

Declaration, 15, 93, 113, 115

Decrement Operator, 28

Delete Operator, 84, 116

Delete[], 80, 84, 87-90, 109, 112, 116, 118, 120

Denis Ritchie, 3

Derived Classes, 76, 78, 113

Destructor, 80, 82, 116

Double, 89, 116

Encapsulation, 2, 69, 82, 117, 121

Endl, 9, 49

Enum, 117

Error Beep Character, 50-51

Explicit, 117

Extern, 118

Extraction Operator, 30

Float, 25, 33, 116, 118

Friend, 118

Functions, 12-13, 15, 17, 19, 52-53, 56-57, 61, 63-65, 74-77, 86, 91-92, 104, 112, 118-119, 121

Garbage Collection, 118

Global Variables, 63, 91, 118

Goto, 119-120

Header File, 8, 14, 19, 91-92, 119

History of C++, 1, 3, 11

Identifier, 22

If Else Statement, 39, 42, 44, 93

Include Statements, 13, 17-19, 55, 114

Increment Operator, 27

Infinite Loops, 46

Inheritance, 78, 80, 119-120

Inline, 119

Inline Function, 119

Insertion Operator, 30

Int, 9, 15, 22-24, 27-28, 31, 33-37, 40, 46, 53, 55, 57, 62, 64, 66-68, 70, 76, 83-84, 87-88, 93-94, 98, 108, 116, 119

Integer, 22-23, 28, 57, 119-120

Iostream.h, 13-14, 16, 30, 32, 92, 114-115

Java, 83

Ken Thompson, 3

Keyword, 35-36, 70, 73, 94, 113-123

Local Variable, 120

Long, 10, 14, 33, 35-38, 83, 91-92, 107, 109, 120

Loops, 24, 35-36, 39, 44-46, 93

Main Function, 14-15, 17, 19, 31, 53, 55, 57, 63-65, 72, 76, 88, 91

Math Problems, 96-97

Matrix Array, 67-68

Memory, 21, 83-85, 87-90, 99, 108-109, 112, 115-116, 118, 120

Memory Address, 84-85, 99

Memory Allocation, 83

Memory Leak, 89

Method, 39, 49, 51, 67, 120

Multiple Arguments, 57, 62

Multiple Inheritance, 120

Namespace, 9, 31, 91-92, 95, 118, 120

Naming Convention, 33-34

Nested Class, 120

Nested Loops, 45

New Operator, 87-89, 120

New[], 3, 22-23, 48-49, 55, 72, 80, 82, 84, 87-90, 109, 112, 116, 118, 120

Newline Character, 31, 48-50

Object Oriented Programming, 2, 4, 61, 117

OOP, 1-3, 46, 74, 77, 82, 121

Operator, 19, 25, 27-28, 30, 35, 46, 72-73, 76-78, 84-85, 87-89, 91, 93-94, 111-112, 114, 116, 120

Polymorphism, 2, 113, 121

Pointer, 83-85, 88-90, 99, 112, 116, 121

Private, 76-78, 112, 114, 121

Program Flow, 35

Protected, 76-78, 112, 114, 121

Public, 74, 76-79, 112, 114, 121

Quotes, 50-51, 91

Remainder, 26, 111

Return, 9, 17, 31, 53, 55-57, 61-62, 118, 122

RTTI, 122

Short, 1, 30, 51, 63, 107, 122

Signed, 122

Spacing, 9-11

Static Object, 122

Strategies, 96

String, 14, 23-24, 28, 31, 33-34, 48-51, 53, 87, 99, 119, 123

Struct, 70, 73, 123

Structure, 70, 72-73, 76-77, 82, 123

Subject Matter Problems, 98

Syntax, 107, 123

Tab Character, 49, 51

Tag, 123

Throw, 123

Unsigned, 123

Value, 21-25, 27-28, 31, 37, 42, 46, 53, 55-57, 62, 66, 68, 93-95, 99, 102, 113, 116-119, 122-123

Variable, 15, 21-24, 28, 31, 33-34, 37, 40, 53, 55, 62-66, 68, 72, 83-84, 86, 88-89, 93-95, 98-99, 113, 118-120, 123

Vector, 123

Vector, 123

Virtual, 112, 122

Void, 53, 55, 62, 108, 119, 123

Warnings, 107-109

While Loop, 39, 44-45, 116

About the Author

Sam has been programming in C, C++, html, and VB for over 5 years. He likes to spend his time away from the computer with his friends. He hopes to one day start his own software development company. His association with computers began at age 12 when his parsents bought him his first PC equipped with MS DOS. You can reach Sam at Sch143434@cs.com.

0-595-18739-0

www.ingramcontent.com/pod-product-compliance
Lightning Source LLC
Chambersburg PA
CBHW051245050326
40689CB00007B/1071